IN DREAMS
OF
DIMINISHED RESPONSIBILITY

Miguel Cullen

Acknowledgements

I'd like to thank the publishers of Shooter magazine, DREICH magazine and Ranger magazine (US) for first publishing poems in this collection, my fellow Odilo comerado, art director and book designer, Alix Janta-Polczynski for the increadibly achieved cover, plus book layout, with the cover, you have the confidence of a Greek oracle, so thank you, my collaborator on these past four books, and for good reason.

I'd like to thank the followers I have on my newsletter, all of you, for listening, and some of the responders, among them, Luke Coppen, Chip Martin, Nick Pearson, Ivar Wigan, Rosanna and Anthony Gardner, Jethro Turner, Ian Thomson, Jonathan Keates, and the others..

Also my brother Domingo Cullen, for all his support and love, love you chubwungo, and to my mother, who is such a fine mother, and my dad, who is an incredible father. Thanks to Camilla Grudova for encouraging the new direction, and for her kind praise of the book formally, as well as James Womack for his amazing words of praise. Also, Zoe Brigley of Seren Books for her endorsement, which sadly didn't arrive in time. George Wyndham for keeping me going and for his quiet encouragement and day job at Special Rider Books and Records, stall 64 Shepherds Bush Market, as well as all the SR family.

Speaking of family, I'd like to thank my amazing family Victoria and Mary, Victoria is my wife and she has long had my back, my heart, and held my hand in difficult moments as well as happy ones. Her incredible poetic vision has changed the entire position of my poetry. My muse. Thank you. And Mary. My family is the love of my life. And they will all have my back. And whenever I'm sad they're always there for me. And I hope you think of your family like that as well. And whenever you want to say something, the one thing I think it's going to be is, 'I love you'.

On my Argentine side, I'd like to thank Teresa Anchorena, my aunt, as well as my aunt Mercedes Cullen for encouraging me. And Fede and Carlitos.

As Yungun said, if I forget you, don't stress me, just correct me — as the great man of my alma mater said, if I may be so loquacious as to be indifferent, or the same as other alumni, 'some games you can't play them twice / so play to win that's my main advice.'

Also, Hysteria Promotions for the sound clip played out of the chip in the back of the book.
It's a clip from a recording of the Hysteria jungle/dnb rave in Leicester on the 16th of October 1998, in Starlite 2001 club.
In it, a firework is let off inside during a DJ SS / MC Skibadee set. The MCs, first Trigga, then Bassman, beg an imagined gunman to put down his weapon. We felt it went perfectly with the shooting that appears in 'Rival Dealer Dream', my poem that it goes alongside at the back of the book.

Poems

For months the heat of love has kept me marching

Robert Lowell, "Dream"

Deeply Stylised Dream

It was in a huge palazzo with golden mouloure and swags and carved drapery on the walls

    empty inside apart from flowers — I kissing a girl

    outside was Jamaica the motorbikers   we're going to rob you

the code word was viper or cobra or

      someone destroyed my artistic master — she, A. who thought she was someone grander, fatter, a female Bacchus

    with arms like purple pythons

and someone has tried to destroy your master , also A., a he, and they went out

     so maybe we were going to be each other's masters

    and there was a horrible   fight

    like men fighting seen by young children

    this depth charge dream   stylised

I think the point was an exceptionalism of the soul

   that was hard and had ridiculous taste

     I was in a series of articulated coaches

   driven by a   coachman

     with the same feeling of slipping into old   acid etched deep grooves

         of

   Italian noble heredity — outside there was a garden

     and a lavender pinneaple with a crown like

huge thistle flowers growing high as two or three metres

   and some people with satirical   buffoonery

   their acid privilege encircling me foamily

  were smelling yellow flowers on acid   their tails over their heads like photographers' cloaks

and it reminded me of me

  of you baby

 trying to protect you from the gluttonous bee

in a trance terribly miniaturising you

  and what engulfed me was not having to worry as much about you

   a flashback to when there were huge predators.

An Illness in the Four Seasons Hotel in NoHi

I'm white as a sheet mitey sheet that old sheet   the posh metal blinds are like a fine bird's plumage or a hundred horizons

you as Peter Quennell, Evelyn Waugh's bete noire   who was actually not a good writer, even though he never wrote, do you know that kind of thing

or you as   Mr Miagi-Do catching the flies with chopsticks out your ars nigiri saying goodbye world just to get the front cover

      you were a superb beast you could see what your mother sees in him

     but he put his back out trying to spend it all - he was never the same again!

     You can have infinite pleasure   *as infinite as your soul*, said the sphinx, *but at the end you must say goodbye to it*

the death dust hourglass passes through on to the bed and the mitey white sheet and while the dust mites aggregate

the mucilage of time or the lice of time like a cascade of keyboard characters, like a sort of Microsoft logo going into cornflakes milk

a barred stave of light   shadow on the wall from the venetian blinds and i walk up them

a false dawn the car lights waver and zzzses off.

Bedsit Land

Paddington, Bayswater, Lancaster Gate, Porchester Place, Queensway hotels
in wedding-cake houses
surrounded by piked railings with flags, like tattered drapery over the fourposter-
portico

they can't make a copy of my key card, so Italian Aliche has to come up with me
with the master, thus
cashing in the latent flirtation adding up with the reception desk between us
and we sit mutely in the lift, both like Semeles dying
when Zeus appeared in all his glory –

There's the girl who took one look at me while holding her McDonald's cup, outside and
said 'This is my hotel?!'
and I summoned up a crusty memory of laughing
at people eating Maccy's in hotel bedrooms
using grabber-tongs to rescue a photo of myself, a parody,
from the fire, like the gadget my mum bought for her dad.
I pick up a Californian lilac from the ground with difficulty, that I gave
you, in your flat by the McDonald's

or Old Mary's cocktail bar off Lancaster Gate, down into a lower-ground
down the stairs you can see candles in pools of wax
this freezing foggy morning, something unswallowable, transitory – for all
the boys and girls from the drained Mediterranean provinces
with their chestnut-mousse puffas with stitching and S&M zip situations,

I slap a chestnut on the back, huge thing, its piking branches, with plastic bags the similar colour
to the sky
and think of our wedding rings, the time that tree has stood
through blazing leaves yellow, and wedding candles, and how love in old age, is stronger as it is felt through
grief

my ring   since lost, said '*HOME*', inscribed in
italics.

Short Story Writer Dream

I had a dream that I was American Psycho living at the top of the American Gardens Building on the Upper West Side   and I was the main character

I was a short story writer sincerely   inspired by what I was doing

and then that would be the catalyst   like a relay race going around   on a really really tight circuit

I had a face like the man on the cover

in that book of the eponymous naaaame   a grey worsted wide chalk striped suit with yellow silk tie

he thought he'd get some really good material for his short stories

by killing someone   so he basically found them stalked them down

he was fatally in love with him the main guy   he was   doing relay passing the baton with himself again and again on the short circuit

he kept thinking of moments when he'd   do   it
write it down

but he couldn't find the right moment

it was like the fictional diary in *American Psycho*   disgusting   the perfect beige- grey-   boudin noir-portrait   with

a face red like an inside out mask of a man not wearing a mask.

Animal Farm Dream

I was with the methyl color   snapdragons   and their dog tongues,   the bees   in their gobs the bee   draining the root   canal

and I was in   tied in by breadcrumb trail   by daedalus the   napoleon drug boar   —   so swift in reasoning   a paragon of animals   bear-baited   withnail speech of mourning

I am a polymer of sargassum   and spasticine off to the   shops   come back as pritt-stick   the aubade or the ballad of   Boxer who misses   un-bait   I   preaching or singing   yehudi menuhin   jewish fiddle   to the   whiling wolves of the 1980s Regent's Park enclosure

boxer   or-well   his pritt-stick lost its cap
and he dare not stick it into   the old mother   sow black cap

so after   being turned to glue   sleeps
it off in rapid squiggly city

Sol LeWitt throwing his wit away   lackaday   wiggling around the coke   straw   like the ass of a wasp   le cul d'une guêpe in a snapdragon

tinkerty tonk, old cuneo   tiddle-oh tiddle-ay   rin-tin-tin   tink-tink-tonk tiddly rink-a-dink   shimmy shimmy ya shimmy yo shimmy ay
chim chimney chim chimney chim chim cheroot

Insert jargon argot patter   insert   feeling of   bonhomie   and roseateness   via anxiolytic anon   indefinite run.

Poem for my Love (Diana and Actaeon)

I had a dream about a woman with dirty foie gras coloured fingers that were dabbed with pearl
rings and her back was rough as if plied with uneven makeup it was a inconsistency of the skin in
the colour of sweet wine and she ended like a mugger at the bottom

        of a spiral stair she was a shockingly attractive woman to all and I was subdued to
    the ranks of many men part – obsequious part – crying ..,sorry

   In the Acropolis museum I associated with Darth Vader   crowing that I was addicted
vaingloriously to wine like Dionysius but that I was the god of it

I invented this so I could invent a pseudonym for you whom i was enraged by by love you
were a Papposilenos D's tutor, m 'tutor I would dissemble gratuitously

I went to him it was to him I went to   account for the balance of the penumbra for the
details of which the rest just was – if as all who are in love do declare - the rest is just details

   and he counted everything that was nothing

        and came back and gave me the figure   and I laughed with happiness – you'll not
   laugh

        that even though we knew the broken-down accounted-for ad-infinitum factored-in
   grand total of   nothing

        I could still wonder at the tooth paste diamond flecks in your guilty grubby louche
   long fingers.

Shame Dream

I had a dream I was Adam revisiting my first garden

      the light was full color vintage 1980s   like when I was a   boy holding a golden thread in his orbic head I wanted to do an   *urbs picta*

    and to unpick the dread of the giovannotto   it was a juvenile   a weakling's   crime   a man-slaughter   we had arrived in this walled city

    seeking permission to enter the garden that was a way away from this   historical town   but I didn't know that yet   in times of yore I had been used as a   child as a cat burglar to break into the garden

    with the black hand to leave no prints on the gun   had shot the owner   to be indemnified of this I was now

by papal bull of Urban I   asked to St Lorenzo of the Escorial   to excoriate

    the pest from the royal rotting rooms as a punishment for my crimes   the *pudridero*   and I was led by my false beliefs to a tunnel from the *pudridero*'s bathrooms that led to my first garden was and so I went in   paid the attendant and dove right through the toilet

    I climbed out of the storm drain in the centro storico   completely covered in sniffer rats

but no prize no garden   just my atonement for my crimes   and I had to lead them out to drown

   in order   to fully serve my penitence   and wore the memory of the rats like an illness like lepers'

bells, tinkling when there are landmines but I planted a bomb once I'd cleaned the gisant   rotting rooms of rats in the *pudridero*   a fuck you for the punishment

    and it blew clean up but i cleaned the rats the sin from those royal bodies

      but now i make my confession to my lord

   I hope not just to visit the garden where I first came as a   gopher assassin in a cat burglary gone wrong – I was not guilty I was five

   ffs   I have lived a life of punishment and have washed sin from many crimes I was too young to be guilty of

   now let me live in the garden.

.

Siamese Dream

There should be a name for cigars smoked by two II year-old kids, given to them by a much older man
in the Bahamas after a cool evening in a beach restaurant
we would split open up the cigar   spatchcock it and fill it with local sensi   butterflied   like a pair of
evil   Siamese twins
 it was all gooey inside   so we thought: fork this!
     and   spread the cigar paper out   like a papyrus there were certain sentences cut out
     we laid it over   a sheet of bible vellum
                    opened at the Second Coming
   and see certain things through the two meshes
                 like a grille cipher   of Turin shrouds:
 a massive ginkgo in autumn its huge yellow the mattness of it   the heart-shape leaf like a pair of con-
joined siblings
        at the obverse of the paper   speckled and flecked like a spitting fire   going out into the soul
     the color of gingivitis gums salt- clouded leather   spam
   -pink   smoky black grape antithetical black   a George Rouoy   painting of gay underhanded wast-
ings of the flower
       the cigar paper was like the sudarium the veronica
     turin shroud again   stars plotting us the right way   rosicrucian ciphers like the Louis Vuitton
pattern and color
in the end our fate was dissimilar
       but there were lots of forking paths a lot   of
       forking paths   fork   that was a fine cigar.

Oral Fixation Dream

he had a dream   a coreless   dream   he was in a   massive   basement of a baronial Alabama plantation
house of his

wife's   with a   gun   a Colt 500 horse-stopper   and he was going to   get   these   huge gigantic
snakes   and it wasn't a joke

they were living rent-free in   these   huge opium dens   with dun coloured

    performative opium   dust   coming out   in pharmacopeia masquerades   creepily   fading
out incompletely

    the snakes were gluttonous eating geckos so he threw them another unclassified   unidentified
reptile

    and he was throwing them a bone ... and it grabbed it and bundled him in their open mouth   and
it was a fiercely   androgynous   erotic   dream

    and afterwards he came out of the snake's ass which was kinda nice

like assertions of primacy in missionary   male-on-male sex acts   in prison   but it felt lovely.

Crucifixion Dream

I went to a vending machine which was like a microwave   put in a coin made of meat and it made me a
burger   it was like being given a compensation for living the meat coin was made
of me

there was a golden apocalyptic light like a pure realisation like   armed 14 year-olds in
Vietnam lords of all Creation doing killing and forgiving   what they wanted   and we were
poor as field mice in the periphery of London going to see healers for living-pain

and this guy Matt he was recouping a debt   fully blown muscular anger   it was bad debt
which I'd accrued for all my mates putting up with my drivel for decades when they just should
have gassed me for being schizophrenic   it was growing beady-eyed   in the dark the debt
falling apart and growing on itself   going very bad

meanwhile I was as well   meat was coming off me like a king's robes with
embroidered veins and paisley drops of pus I stank terribly I grew to regret it as   though it
suited me   it didn't suit him

and he sent me to the asylum   to buy some more time   he got the algorithm to notice me
and   to get me well for the valuation well   you'll see

I didn't want to   disclothe too much incase it made him madder but he was ambivalent and
held my

unfolding drapery like a sycophant or vaguely giggling small satyr   and inveigled me
into shorting my death   so I would die quicker and profit in the underworld
cleaves of meat falling off the nerves eating into me like ants

and this was bad   I was addicted to medicine vended also by the machine
as the PTSD was unpredictably   attracted to the medicine and I would scream about being covered
in ants when it was not really a worry in the asylum   the debt accrued   unchecked

and Matt faked my death   not before outsourcing quants who hedged it so hard the price
rose on my head

and I kept being told   in the golden apocalyptic light like a 14 year- old beautiful Leonardo
DiCaprio in Vietnam   firing a chain-feed chugger

I kept being told that I had died there and I kept dragging myself on

and they found a rave where there was a Resonance FM playing 87 on the fm dial   a pirate
and I was burger meat only   that

and they were talking at the rave how once I died the hedge-fund money from shorting my
life would help pay off the bad debt from my psychosis   and I recorded them with your phone
Vic but just recorded the pirate radio

lol   and I thought you'd like   that

and I gave the   proper chavs who were on the BBQ at the rave the rest of me to grill
proper cat meat pocked thinly spread   burgers for the squat pirate dance   an unbearable
feeling like   death   or Vietnam.

Low Blood Sugar Level Dream

I had a dream I was Ray Winstone and I was being chased by some bad gang some big cunts some nazi
bitches a   guy called AK 47 a dreadlocks and his wife Brunella they chased me   from
Elephant & Castle to Wood Green   which wasn't very green   it was a forest of topsy turvy
asphalt ivy

I was Irish as the Irish were the toughest in NYC   and the Irish were a friend of the Jamaicans and being
Argie is like being Irish among the Blacks in the UK   anyhow I was up against the final bosses

some Spanish yardies who sold crack on the riviera and there was a coffee shop on the first floor of a liv-
er-coloured council estate – it was the first one I'd seen … ironically …

I was now being chased by Ray Winstone – I was Rocky Balboa ….. Probably

and I was on my tummy like a fish   big cemetery   in Lima in drawer-like coffins – and he got a
manual corkscrew and pulled out all my innards – through my mouth first my heart and my knee caps –
then my guts –
                    so I was   an empty man – which caused me much
        resentment and I couldn't die because if I died I would go to hell so I had
        to stay alive so I could be good and go heaven but my body died

                    I was in hell and it was claustrophobic like a cling film   bag with
        bust-ups with more rudeboys but as hell was evil it had a weak character
        so I slim-jimmed my way out so I was in the real world again it was
        incredible

but the pigs gave chase – they caught up quick – but as I had given the government or charity 23
mill in my will

I was spared jail.

Betrayal Destiny Dream

Went on holiday with Rory and Jill there was quite a thing between you two   but I didn't feel like
going into battle for you
and you were mortally wounded either took offense or by her I think it was the former
Brian and Pete and BK they were watching the glossy headlights in the rain going in a cab
they were   parodying
        my   engrossed sensitivity to my privilege   and I said   'drive I'll alight here'   and they
laughed   between the Blantyre Estate in Chelsea and the
garage with the two cars with 2BE and NOT2BE registrations
      they surprised me   with a no-expense spared bender in a pub with   fruit machines not Vegas
          and a house dealer and it was abstruse a bar freezer full of ancient proverbial Chinese
eggs   like a book of parables and riddles
          and they said mate you'll die if you carry on like this and we'd love to get fucked w you but
you've got to stop smoking
and it was really nice   then we were late for a flight to a vale of health   like it was   for a retrieval of
our
 youth   and we were sliding down the escalator bits to get there in time and Pete was really
abusive to people who were wearing veils
like Emirates   stewardesses and we were detained for what seemed an age
    I   knocked the hat off somebody who was moralising at me he ended up having a cake tin of
weed residue under it and I said gleefully
you got weeeeeeed!!! and we gained plaudits and were freed and
boarding school makes you wanna drink so all the people you make friends with just wanna get
drunk.

Deep Mourning Dream

Pete   I had a dream you were doing a reverse Circle Line pub tour   that all   prefects at Eton had to do by

   having a birthday-party   rave crawl in small industrial estates all around London in little tents over the estate pub   yards   ending in Paris at Napoleon's tomb

       there was a morbidity to the objectification
   of the working class of   rave   of aristocracy   of   ghettoisations   which had an endpoint

   what kind of person would write poems like these   the same kind of person who would

masturbate after beating his partner   it's not a good
   dream to have so we had to get out of that

and the dream was a rave crawl   but it was a reverse rave crawl   I had really a sense of it being a mourning   so

   we were wearing outré birthday suits for a celebration   smoking fake chalk -dust cigarettes

like a mockery of the king that he esteemed as essential

       a rave   without race or beliefs or love or hate

pure element.

Jetlag Dream Night Two

    I had a reverse dream   about the very late night Jamaican speakeasy   like the one in St
Paul's in Bristol   just above   the Charing Cross road Leicester Square tube entry   it
reminded me of every
    dream I've had every dream is the same dream it had carrying- on secret passages across that were hard
to break into like
    crews or birth canals the texture
of   organ tissue   it was like the squat by the westway   café Ravenous   wII and the
cloakroom had people going up and down like a canalicular dam   waterfall
    I had to unhook my meat carcass   back from the cloakroom   take two coins back and put
them back into my daughter's pocket money purse   like the plot entrusted to me
    I couldn't remember the rest of the plot   and I couldn't clench like a fist after waking up
instead of movement in air —   water
    I was surfing on top of trains at a very busy train junction like in deepest Brazil third world
industrial trains on   deep drugs   like crack which caused lesions
    there was a gypsy encampment in the middle of all the train lines   the original entity   which
despite its locality was entered via the poshest hotel like a mandarin oriental in hong kong   but now a
deeply low plateau-ed   resort-hotel for
    the brickworks labourers for all the arts & crafts capitalist over-par ghettos   Welwyn
Letchworth   and it was like like   time   and the accumulated bric a brac of   society's
sausage-meat belt-conveyor passages   highs and lows   diagonals
    I could reach this gypsy market where I was buying souvenir gifts for a variety of mistresses
    I was looking for a poster that was like a plastic sheet   and I found one that was a
MenaceIISociety film flag and some cool ultra retro saturated remastered   *Trainspotting* dark
mood-pic throws
    and Pete was guilty in perpetuity for this crime he'd invented in   his head like a battery
that was leaking   battery   acid aciiiiiiiid
    and the way out of the sentence was to follow the vision. But putting it on   the dream was
difficult   to avoid the mistakes   I made with you Mary
   when   shitting out my   complexes   it was ghastly how the punishment was so near.

<u>Gay Dream</u>

there was a boy who had hairs all over his breasts   they were tiny he was orphaned by his flat
chestedness   he thought he had all-over moles

   growing hair   when it was cigarette burns smoking   still   he was so fucking flat chested
even his hole was small   his penis was like a diamond backed python it would swallow people
right up

   straight men and gay men both love anal as it is like profligacy which never ends either   they
are famished orphans   atrophied by their wife's omnivorousness and want a shelter   either
but not or boasting of their own femininity and that's not all   men have special gifts like anal
glands

   with a whiff of this if they wear makeup and poof ! They're gone like a gay wizard   gay men
always evert their anal gland sacs with other men they find attractive   it's a gaydar — it's
deliciously confusing   mixed with women's perfume

   and you could say I'm homophobic by I just know the perfume   eau de   cul de sac

   I've swallowed it and I've been swallowed

   and I've been ok.

Repressed Homosexual Dream

I am writing an article for *Dazed & Confused* magazine and this editor was a natural baby-type   with amazing skin like FKA twigs showing me

 I should distrust everybody with an imperfect PH because this was very deeply obscene and the password to being a baby was very long and I couldn't cope with it very well so

I had a dream that I was with a guy in a coloured room and the only thing he could have was men

and he felt the full force of his all-encumbering sexuality and despite this he wanted to detach gay feeling from it so they became fully transitioned into women and he placated himself that he liked porn, which was basically transitioned people

         but unearthing it he wanted to fuck guys but did not   allow his dream to be like that

but with a condom because he was wary of STDs and they said ok   laughing

there were lots of them in the same room and one who was a bad girl tranny   who was trying to get the nest to realise he wasn't who he was pretending to be and it was giving him deep sickly unease

 in a obscene halo of daylight the colour of a *Deerhunter* bamboo lodge

and   all the Thai kids were hiding in a cupboard but wouldn't shift like bats who had early gender realignment he was horrified to think he was implicated

they were really high up in the English country house and he felt it was incumbent upon him to do something

he was trying to get them down but the pulley the ropes kept thinning out and just   trailing around this was a   South American   pulley

Robert de Niro turned up really good at shooting he shot a swan that came out catastrophically from a big herded flock

     and said *who's the real bad guy now,* like someone saving him from being gay like a redeemer now

     in uncertain cultures he's seen as God, giving us a warning, uncreating his world

      to show us his unfulfilled potential   and how all

of this could affect us negatively.

Instagram Poetry Dream

and maybe I'm getting a little rusty but she's like court jesters   gown that was tied up at the neck and then floated down   a mime artist

she was like a mime artist wearing a sheet and a black Venetian mask with hands with the thrown off pathos of elephant trunk-tips like a sketch   Matisse

she would mime success her gown would hide   the perishable flesh was in last place in her bestiary hierarchy the last recognised or prioritized by her costumier or couturier

she was working at a Fashion Week very strong eye for details   only thin people   fitted through the key they were like keys that fitted   she had a monopoly   was above the people who handle *Paper*'s instagramming because she was posting it before like a hand   of cards

getting VIP in a nightclub is like black magic   you can't get it if you're rich or have a good job

they are the top nobody else. And she's posting it,

like a mime playing charades and the right answer is a sex orgy   as a sting

operation posting only to the people on her private instagram with the viewers restricted to only two with eyes-only access

and if you want to be happy you mime success or mimic the mimers of success maybe it won't happen and then you'll want to die you've, either lied to yourself if not others or, b. ignored the secret to happiness which is not to compare yourself to others

wearing loads of make up so she could look thinner stuff that accentuates your cheek bone and takes away your chin

working in fashion it's a form of purity like purely ornamental Kuba textiles from the Congo or Matisse cut-outs no jolts   no mask no conspiracy theories congregating around the space inbetween   pure aesthetics and the beauty which is numbing humbling

and terrifying.

<u>Punter Dream</u>

I dreamt I was going to a pearl-dealer and the pearls were in a big conch like a gravy boat terrine
above   an old pull-chain water closet with china pink and blue colors

  and he was   selling his body and I wanted to buy   and when you sell your body it means a
great deal to the person buying it but nothing to the person selling it and it   can be very
profitable for the person selling it

          being a punter is like being an   aristocrat selling your immensely aged   estate
after the end of an entailment   you want to very much but would pay a large amount of tax
after   in disfiguring pain

and   it's normal to want to sell your body to the homeless

  it could mean so little to you   but would mean so much to them

      in a cheap hotel with single and double beds in the same room bedspread the colour of
autumn kaleidoscope themes

  inches from the walls and white plastic wrappers around the toiletries and a cling film sleeve
over the upside down plastic cup

    so at the pearl-dealer's I asked him to use the bathroom   to try on some of the pearls

    and left alone I reached around above the cistern and stuffed them all in my pockets and
wanted to leave him a string in of pearls   like the gesture reckless courtly disrespectful to
the establishment a line of blow   on the porcelain

          but didn't.

Based Dream

I'm in Chichen-Itzá watching the total eclipse on mushrooms
    and the dragonflies are really cool
        glowflies like   popcorn with corduroy outlines
    a guy who looked like an albino the Weeknd made of polymer
    driving a perfect car
     listed with you my unbelievable defects
  he had some sort of skull leant forward as his figurehead
        and I was in the back in a Burgundy ribbed leather seat for one
        I guess you were talking to yourself
    the dream was a gun with no recoil a nostalgia
        with no total
                recall   a dream
        with no meaning no morning
            a day with no wind   a dark with no black
  o with no round   xanax with no back-across
    no holes just blank volume no   consequences
            no consolation no pain   no forces
        an empty receiver with no alarm
        your eyelid is a feather headdress
            making tomahawk eyes
        at me
    no stop no go
   and the carved-in   plinths in the tube r
    going aaaaaaaaaaaa   like the jaws of skeletor in Grayskull castle
        and the   gel-grey table-top
    has the depth of the accreted weakness of the flesh
     of the religious sculptors
            the droplet of phlegm that
        makes   the work ambiguous.

Glassed-In Dream

        the moon was a nenuphar a waterlily it was a bud

and the roots would go way down
                    where we were

looking up at the surface turgid waterflies would sit on it
it wasn't very warm where we lived   and we kept banging on the glass to see the moon

           we tried every ruse caught a bat skimming the depths with an angling line

so when he spreadeagled himself in the moon we could bring it down with us

we tried messing with the hose that was in the water sucking on it hard
so the waters would swell and the moon would cosy up to us then we fucked it up in the face

we tried thrashing our gills like morse code reflectors so the moonwalkers would pick it up and the
looper moths came and surrounded our pond like   ripples around a flickering lightbulb

           but the harrier hawks never came to lift us up the great white tiburóns
       flexing from the depths like me cletus, fredo and grizelda

           writhing in the gorgeous clasp of king-raptor-wraiths

           breaking the meniscus with a glorious blast whumping its wings

under which we fell in hiding from God

Illiterate Son Of A Proust Expert Dream

The best was punching mingo i had two broken hands from punching   one eye closed trying to
ride a horse with two broken hands so

we tried to take a cab but were denied and he claimed we had assaulted him he left us at a
family's

house while the cops came and we were trying to stop him from   breaking all the artworks
at the   painter's house they were all charlatans selling snake oil

                    the more they said   the higher the price of their art went — artists are all
            charlatans   that kind of artist   he scrubbed the faces off a
            maggie hambling portrait of an old woman

                    and i was in their swimming pool   and I couldn't get any purchase it
            was just water

I was on a horse holding the reins through my fist that was broken and the artist's mother
suggested i did something scornful dilating about mourning in the French proust's style

    and i gave it ago why not everybody might

but it came out vertically like a pictogram poem by apollinaire sous le pont mirabeau

                                        the little words like incongruous little ciphers that
revealed the further beauty of letters   like algebra where all the   letters have values   maybe
this proust was the exception that proves the rule that all books are wrong

    so I beat her challenge   and i used the book to towel my broken fists and it was written in tiny
illegible grains of sand that intercommunicated with each other softly something i could not do
                    and i boxed with the sandpaper

and scrubbed away all the faces off the walls all your faces intercommunicating like the skill of old
masters conveying singing in cannon i got the whole of it and took it off the walls.

Broadwater Farm Sex Dream

I had a dream I was on a train   pudgy my skin lizard like   pads   pale against the glass rocking a
cross my eyes swollen to slits   it was like   I was narrowing them   but I'm just beat up   my
voice is like I'm sneering but it's just ...

    there was this busker wearing masses of chains   a mad max avirex with a hells' angel

with a broken   wing   my teeth were grainy and sharp like a saw making my tongue sore   and
spotty   our chains got tangled   so

we got off together   at Broadwater Farm there was a skate bowl there

below the overpass you could see it through the disappearing slit   you were like Cedalion the dwarf on
the shoulder of Orion   conducting me

    broadwater it slips off the tongue in a west indian accent there   this pink dressed girl from
east
    asia bumped past me saying excuse me! excuse me! in a chimaican accent

    then (in my dream) we went home and I spasmed as she whipped me with the hair on her
head   it was blatantly beautiful

    like seaweed   that dark orange and litmus paper alkali brushing away from me

    like time. Attack ships on fire off the shoulder of Orion. Time to die.

Depreciating Retro Dream

we were in an ugly rectangular ocean, the ocean floor was see through   and at the tip of a tower block

                  somewhere to the left you could see   crops of very tall autumn trees below us like from Richmond Hill

      there was a lightning storm there Matt was saying ,

    down in the real bit there's lightning

signifying something a bit horrific,   like class   the underworld coming to take us

      and Matt said

      we better shut the windows — in case it electrifies the water and the whole system and Matt he laughed

      making me uncomfortable   sounding   pompous,   so sees it sadly through the windows of the glass with water

      and Giacomo Gaetani was a psy trance editor at the Wire mag cos he knew so much from going to School

      there was at a big birthday party for all the people we went to school with

with Giacomo Gaetani   the coolest   was sub editor for the Wire

      with a small the

      I wanted to get a job writing about poetry for the Wire mag

a column

    about poets, ancient like trendy ones from the 1980s

    and   you used to have a repetitive dream about   being in a flotation tank living   with parasites

        and Giacomo was not over it   he was holding an auction at Christie's on the champion parasites and   buying up ones after undervaluing them

        Atlantis a huge underwater palace   sealed off in a time warp   covered in coir quite dry

and basically if people forget about you they don't think they're better than you, but that you're not part of their world anymore, just left out

with a ocean fish tank on stilts with feasting tables and parasites

and they just think you're not a part of their world

which is understandable given the grandeur of everyone's world,

and Giacomo   was under my shirt sucking at me
vaguely   satirising   himself to the king   only very vaguely   as if he was messaging him something, to resign

and   I was surprised   but understood that he would be king and felt well

that   he stayed so long, as I had felt so fat   and was happy with myself for being so

noble   about the prestige.

Holocaust Dream

the footage of the parody was deeply deeply   aged

        in a landscape was a   strangely shuffling   Orthodox Jewish Russian man   with soft
soft

locks with no hat and full hair — his nails were weathered oxidized scalpels   with white edges
we were all fighting against him   he looked like Dostoevsky

mixed with a little bit of Abraham   talking to his Abramovich   on the mount

   his   long hair and wild and

    the feeling of being beaten   while he was   wailing   prophesying   what he was
going to do —

 and we were in a black world with white slaves in the fields   in ghettos run by wanton white
rude boys

            it was the end of the world   deeply thick   the same as now   it was like he
prophesied

and the question was   whether we could withstand
the whole   punishment

   the footage was grainy   with glass splinters   different   ricochets   whining like mosquitos

 my brother was there   we   were

        listening to music through headphones Radiohead   drone

        skin ingrained   with tiny shrapnel and lice,

wandering around.

Old Therapist Yearning Dream

I was with a female assassin and she was watching us take ourselves apart like beautiful solid silver machine guns

  the whole thing and each part   was all delineated understood   and the gun

was benign like a Brannen-Cooper flute and each

piece was solid silver and had its own cleverly designed   compartmentalised empathy for both the unity and the individual pieces

It was me, me ex therapist and her son S   she was a bit impatient at her son

she was having a cigarette while he was   taking himself apart she   tapping her foot a little bit

as I told her about my week   and they were beautiful musical instruments   that could be unscrewed

    made of silver a very difficult flute or wind instrument

She was like Dr Spurr my old housemaster   a perfect   Italophile

  sense of classical proportion

   and it was a rare happy dream.

Nouveau Riche Dream

        I had a dream two lesbians   were lying on top each other knees in between each others' legs

and then lying beside each other legs crossing

they were going together to a summer wedding and they were embarrassed because they hadn't told any-
one they were gay

—   one was white and one was black wearing a disguise of sunglasses

that were gold only the size of pills held together delicately

        they were in a   teenage bedroom lit by a deep green see-through blinds and a lamp

    and the whole was for the tediousness of the administration that slows life down

      mainstream, normcore, corecore,

   and the women wanted to do a comb Spanish style in their hair   but didn't know how to
install it

  with a black privacy curtain like a old-style photographer

     looking at you through a magnifying glass   horrifically magnifying you so you were
bigger than houses

   to him — and yet from such a tiny physical entity.

        and the girls they were twins in the dark and I was there and they were
interchangeable

    and they swallow they're identical in that way.

   the tiniest things that seemed so large

  taking huge revenges for the smallest acts.

Deeply Acculturated Dream

Walking through a wavering field of   nostalgic macabre   tweeds

if you have money you can have gout it's ok because your tweeds are tailored

fox-fur brilliantine seaweed   in a golden graveyard inside a palace

And one of them said her fur was made of nose hair the other one was made of female pubic hair

He began to say just the things he didn't want to say at the right time for time,   heightening heightening

heightening horrific

big room like the Invalides all golden like

tweed doesn't hurt when you lose your leg from smoking weed because it's all tailored

the flap isn't just sewn shut, and you don't cut the leg off anyway you just sling it over

your shoulder like a continental soldier

There was a lovely black girl, an albino communist jewish girl from Stoke Newington

Having sex she was lovely pregnant –

the father used to do security for a reggae sound system

my father walked past the servant who fitted his head down in the round of the entrance bureau

it made him think the manservant had committed suicide

he felt all the way around his temple in case he'd shot himself – because he was so ashamed

about the albino girl

felt all around the temple as if he was in love with him

he said to him to see the family therapist, as if it was the one thing that he really cared about, him

He wrote it down in special writing, old fashioned   writing, tiny cramped, gothic, the numbers were gothic

   he said it was like a frost in the morning

all he was trying to do was to sleep thinking stiffly — uneasily

too much snuff — makes your fingers gold —

walking across the repetitive dream about

cows that looked like rhinoceroses or hippos

but had a fondness for me

so wouldn't charge.

Primordial Ritual Poem

       we were living with misers where   excessive continence had become a kink where
         in the US   where
we counted every second we had to ourselves
     hoarding that too with special counting machines on   our phones   were covered in
microscopic maggots and   zits we pressed that came   in tiny hard orgasms
       We were working at a religious magazine
          there was a priest who was the editor
said pain was   endogenous   original in us
     and not to
mind when he cold- knocked after dark
     and they made us write books about bo-peep and the passion of the lamb
      under mean time constraints   in   big slave collars   and my friend made a
speech at
  at an all-boys club   and all my female family were the only members except for William he
had married a nonentity

and   it   the speech   was written in the fever of   high emotion   and nobody clapped
    so I clapped harder but I couldn't
   resuscitate the clapping
    and   he as a consequence was getting
wrecked saying he felt   incredible but I knew it wasn't true
       &   there was a friend an old friend that I can't forget and he had like a professional
aristocrat in his family   —
    impoverished,
      and he had an idea for us all to cook   for them on holiday   in China — they were wearing nehru
collars the women in dutch-missionary dresses   and he wanted us all to take each other
   to shreds with kung fu knives for
    sashimi on ice for the count's touristic experience
     otherwise if they thought it was disgusting to eat human sushi   he could wear our shreds
on a gown for big   pearlescent sequins   at the   ball
    holding incense sticks in mock-samurai demonstration ways   dancing to psy trance
        and I   with the same knowledge I have now   was questioning the sexuality of it
all,
      the trees all male   all really   bonded
 a pinnacle a kind of high gross style
    in the   monastery in northern China   which
is so unemotional the sea   froze.

Jetlag Dream

I had a dream I was in the low   ceilinged   hostelry   riven   with tentacular   fire shadows
        and you   guys   were wearing   shooting hats   and your faces were veal   skin   dabbed in
crimson   and blue velvet   beauty spots
        with mustard (French)   cravats made of   felt   it was a dream cast   and impregnated
with   a beauty   that burnt us up
        then I was in   a newsagent it was see-through   with fires burning   strangeness   the
colour of the wine on a white bread basket
 a lapsed   oldness controlled in space   like a broken leg filled with pins   at the newsagent
waiting for   a ticket   at the foot of the castle
    I was going through the usual stop sign   but the feeling was of protection
        a torture garden that gave me what I needed and was like a microcosm that stopped
me murdering people for real   — I don't know if you know
        —   it was then I was with Skepta and Ray Liotta and they were shaving his body like
conscripts'   heads in *Full Metal Jacket*
    and he had so much hair on his body   they were shearing it off like he was a huge beastman
and his wife a bimbo albino
        with some neutral gear   in the   deep-hipster   commune
    in the postwar zone   which is now   just peace
    the sex parasite was   the stanchion struts   were crabs laying eggs   in the roots of the
pubes   it was an albino   eating   Evian   who knew his willy was lazy it was always at half
mast   in the economical movement
of what was old given over newly to poverty   — Robert De Niro was carving a crater into the
bullet nubbin and filling it with pigs blood like the yardies   sealing it loading it
        so you get infections from the wounds   non-Ital   dread-liquidator   Medusa wet-boy.

Smoking Dream

there was a boy covered in   hair   around his breasts

from   a mole that covered his whole chest   it was as if his chest was bruised and exuding smoke
through the skin

the   cowled saliva ducts by his frenulum
seemed to be crying   he wore his odor of stale smoke

like a non finito sculpture   partly entombed in marble unfinished   the   raw flesh

his teeth were like lilies dotted with profligate orange pollen

cappuccino cigarette filter orbits   with chocolate sprinkles   I dread nought but dare not see
what the message

is in the held velvet   gloves painted with deft aplomb   what flower is in your hand   —

the foxglove   lung   all marbled on the inside   endpapery

gloves filled with digitalis   lilies splattered with blood pollen my body gives it to me and i spurn
your flowers so it rages   throwing down

its gauntlet   and gives you something real   to cry about.

Affluencer Dream

I part-dreamt omnivorously the cedar trees' skin were a hysterical white
          the colour of fire kindled by wood whittled down

          he was a white guy with arty   pigmentation-loss   and had   naturally   brown hair
in the same way as   if he had had green hair there was an   unstoppable   irregularity to

him that was   so   programmed in him that   other people   felt it indelibly and

his emotions were so   unintelligible   that they were   soft and smooth like an old stone

          and there was another   as well   with huge ginger freckles the size of big polka dots on
his white face

    and loads of soft really really long bumfluff on his face   aged 24   and   black nipples

          there was a faulty Argentinean political figure who had cobra-poison instead of blood

          and his wife used nerve agent and was a spy with a Polaroid camera for the Chinese

          they travel in a new driverless Smart car that can park sideways and has a four seater
cabin all facing conference style in white felt.

          but the wood leaving the multi-storey car park is a worry for the car robot as the wood is filled
with deer.

Child-Star Exile Dream

I had a dream about a gazouillement of oiseaux

    I was the gas and coal prince   owner of one of the only privately-owned oenological chateaux Sezincote

    and Matt wanted to store his wine in my chateau cellar   I was newly teetotal   even to the blood in my veins   this fabled vintage   that was like an old family's blood   I was allergic but it was running in my veins   so I was in anaphylactic shock   so he had taken it over

    had turned it into a really rank members club like 5 Hertford St or Oswald's the snobbiest club masquerading as a wine buff's club

    and changed the keys   and wanted to charge me for him storing his wine in my cellar   as he owned it   but I couldn't understand that this was a complete role reversal   and we kept trying to avoid the really suave manager

    by mistake trying to disturb this imperturbable   man like a nervous tic of ours we kept trying to avoid paying our bill   and the finery

    it was unfortunate   that we kept   tripping over it   and making a red wine mess   and pouring white wine all over it   and we couldn't pay the bill

    and I had another a bit too much   dream that when I was young I had been a child star playing a young MJ in *Moonwalk*   but this hallowed memory was   concealed   by my parents having such big egos

    and I kept having flashbacks of my early adulthood of me wearing the perfect Nike Air Tech Challenge IIs and jean sleeveless overcoats at a perfect bagginess Ecko   monochrome smoky marbling

    jeans at a perfect slackness Armani metal eagle below the bum full curve while still tight in places

    I kept trying to cover up the evidence   or come up with the evidence   I was trying hysterically to become him again   trying to be cool

    and I had the original tape   I wanted to be a child star again   to be adored   objectified innocent echoes

    no one asked the child star if it   would be good for it to be a child star.   It was never improperly supervised.

Coke Dream

I was watching an art-nature film   of him   an elephant covered in black muddy   creepers
all covered in black tusks   it was poached

   the elephant was black   a reverse pigmentocracy   was taking place   where blackest black
is the pinnacle   and

   white was a benchmark for depravity   there was   kind of a hog   coated in coarse mud
his hair was like   lianas of black tobacco   originally he'd had   blond hair like a white
man   or a pig and so it was said

  he had a floppy horn that sagged and sucked in, everted   we were in the undergrowth   the
footage was rough   damaged   maybe it was the trees

the elephant had me and it was feeding me in with its trunk

hoofing me up like powder angry because it had been eating wood   and after   the elephant
was weary so, so so so weary.

           Wet clay on   me like   ass- shit then resin-coloured flies   shading us   from the
dangerous heat   our depravity had predators   so much shame

  and ego—   danger,   a pack of missionaries crawling up out   at the dead stately estancia   in
the fetal   position

        mamáma – my grandma was   still alive   in the day-bed in the salita and her scent

of gingivitis   and lipstick   she had been alive all this time

very old,   lying in state alive very aged, very very gaga   she was barely saying
     'don't wear bow ties   when you have to go out'

    I said ok grandmama   she was wearing a long Chinese flat black dress   pearls   coya
skin pale stretched out like in a tannery

my father reproached me with the furtive regretful   humid eye

   as he had stolen her from the grave to play   like a puppet

   and   when I said   she was not really part of our family dynamic anymore –

  he was sad as he loves his dolly   very much and didn't want to stop making love to her.

And there were clouds of very vivid flies

and they made me a big cowboy hat of a palest used green chewing gum   brim folded up the
sides   but he put it sideways on my head like Napoleon

a mistake, an improvisation they were playing and decided to put it on my head. We went for a
walk and went to see her in her house —

    suddenly the day went   yellow   winter-day   yellow and on dirty peroxide-yellow pampas
there was a

wailing and yip-yipping and the Pampa Indians death squad came   into the plantation

   they had Vic   , she   sat with Mary   on a beige tawny sofa on wheels led by pickups of
the raiding party

 and her man whooping, was her brave, and who was going to have my head.

Detached Repression Dream

the most unfriendly school hero   Horace Capello has a pet hamster he keeps in his tailcoat pocket and he lets him out

in the smoking shed, his cream luxury cashmere jumper has deep-fake torn holes for the thumbs that look perfect with his whole style

he fondles it, lets it run through his fingers from his sleeves and lets you hold it if you're cool

and the only meaningful thing about abandonment-life is a landscaped stately garden

the view   blackened with eerie deep-winter mist,   a horror flick or a crime series like *A Touch of Frost* that   turns senile people back on

and he eats the hamster lets it down his esophagus like a coke condom so it comes back up like a mole in his arse

he has had so many of them go missing he doesn't know

what's going on, who's talking   he says the evilest things

that's the difference between clever perverts like me and careless ones like you   he said rinsing in the bathroom mirror

while I smoke out the window in the toilet cubicle

he falls asleep at night   so asleep he seems anaesthetised   in the school sanatorium in the san

and they push them out

the body just excretes them. The head is plastered up, oblivious.

Eton Bullying Dream

I had a dream i was in a sushi restaurant in a Serbian old-town

    eating a dim sum that had a black interior

    i was in a wheelchair   and people kept walking away from me and I was left on
my own

I was in a room that had strobe on the
whole time like a torture just a blank

    and the boy who came out from where he had been lurking

        and started to say things that made me itchy

            he stood up with a magnificently gallant way and began a story
that he swished about his mouth and it made me wet

    like he had rats on leashes and they were sniffing around

    my crotch and making me so uncomfortably edged and he kept pulling
them away and then letting them back in

        it was like the strangest fetish. It broke down the barrier of
whether i was complicit or passive

    and i was just a lump of organic matter   and he was leaning over me

I couldn't leave

    he was such an impressive
        top-end bully and I began to weep.

Adoration Dream

In over my head   I smell   sour rubbish

carry the   colossal bags   like   a Titanes en el Ring   wrestler   holding in

the secret that it's all fake   coming as a semi-dressed lesbian in nude-coloured bandages
and a meat mask   in the dream I cannot   satisfy   the audience

and with   terrible mournfulness   un-bandage myself to reveal   an engrossed   slouched
creature with a louse-like   armour   with   abnormally microscopic hands

like a gluttonous   person who is guilty of a murder but didn't go to jail   who   can't stop
talking   garrulously and has nervous tics but who stutters

and in their final shell of bandaging   his arms and legs were like a spider diagram covered

in a fleece   of maggots a sheep   frock of white insects   they were eating him   being
carnivores ...

like this catwalk model in a McQueen robe   with
sheer lace tied gathered all up on horns on the head of the model

where the designer is

dealing with themes of excrescence and of   gorgeous things   being abandoned to the
feral abscesses engendered by   social media

and the   sheer cream lace held up by horns on the head of the model

coddled   by microscopic spawn and   phagocytes   that eat the bacteria   and all the
models were being   ruined   tarnished and the   design was eating into their skin and   there was a
furore

and the insects were swollen and it turned out they were pubic – pubic,   lice   and the
models had created a sublime smell they adored and it made them feral.

Illustrious Grandfather Dream

Had a dream about you and me and the Saudis
together we were trying to take over   Mayfair again
but the alliance was shaky   and
accusations flew
 he had Halloween moth
wings inked on his throat
his bow tie knot was like a broken butterfly   fumbled knot
he was sitting in the dated hotel dining room a de-dyed pink
-carpeted
slightly on the edge of things
you had a wasp-waist waistcoat   black
      that's all I can recall

Ejection of Hereditary Peers from the Upper Chamber Dream

I was in the ghetto the colour of a beam of light caught in a silty river   the cabbie was claudio caniggia

who was taking me to the locos and it was warm winter and the water was tepid like the air

I was the difference between corrupt and rotten

because the thing about being Argentinean is that you are metal so you can't rot but you can be corrupted   as we all know sallow skin like plucked   duck

the locos wanted to do a longterm kidnapping, have me in their family and have kids with me and then be assured of the money

like in *Killers of the Flower Moon* where they marry into money, as Emperor Maximillian invented

and we are at kidnap-school and in chapel no one could fit in my pew because I was so marvellously heavy with the smell of sorrow and rubbish

pete and tony had been smoking crack and were incredibly tired from the rave at portobello

the pew candles flickered innocently the huge semi-arc of the dark chapel they had thick hoops

on their crewneck football tour jumpers adulterated by wear into shagginess

I hadn't slept and felt so lonely in my pew on my own and my housemaster didn't pet to see me there

there was a ghostly atmosphere in the ante-chapel with the diaphanous flags of red and gold

the old swimming pool en-bushed and the synthetic green of them and the clear-as-crystal water

the edwardian pool the rain falls on it like stabs in my heart i think of you

the old lords ejected from the upper house   new lords living in them passing new laws

  Live Within The Law And You Will Be Free

only i didn't think your voice could dial it to a pitch so frighteningly low.

<u>Old Money Dream</u>

He dreamt he was on holiday in a cottage in the UK with some friends with old Louisiana plantation money

   we we were sitting   outside   the grey gold

     trophy room   surrounded by imported crumbling masonry from England   and

     the whole house moved from England in splendid decrepitude   the furniture had been lost but

     he'd bought it back from a myriad of different parties and he fed the furniture to the house as if it was hungry

except it wasn't   it was   not   alive

    with the sagging plaster damask Grinling Gibbons ceiling

     that gave way five times a day under the crystal chandelier each time they rebuilt it more decrepitly

   and   one of the brothers went missing

and nobody could be bothered to find out where he was – on the run   or kidnapped or just drifting they just

    left it   and he might have been in the closet or he was just concealing his wealth   it was more or less the same

    and when he confessed the family trustees giggled unstoppably

    and it was like a flood of blood coming like *The Shining* all over all the house

   Human life is evil and only on earth and not for long.

Ballad of Sexual Dependency Dream

misers are misers because they only see their worth in their objects   because they have no self
                                                    worth

   I was never a plausible hunter   I would like 'walking-up' to scare the birds and wait for
one to fly over

When I was objectified at a very young age it gave me my bloodlust,   when I became a very
highly sexed teenager it added to it I swapped

a catapult for a shotgun   it was too easy

   I would see myself in dirty objects of desire   like the flea-ridden buzzards I would bring down   they
would smell of death   I had a dream I was guilty of a murder the closest I ever
got was

lady killing   I lived in a hall of horns   of skins imagine a rug made of a woman with the head

       the biggest trophy was atrocious   in the hunt   it hunted me   like an animal that
was absurdly uniquely at the top of the food chain   even me with my guns.

       I am a ragged bull   like bait underwater its   fronds abradedly   absent mindedly
stroking the water   bitten away sharks

       a thousand tiny fish lick my   locks of white brambled meat   I feel temporarily
comfortable in my hall of mirrors each one a dirty porno with me

   it mothers   me   now I cut you in half and reveal you in integrity   my wife is a criminal
and we   don't hurt each other   she's in the mob.

Mystery Farter Dream

Had a dream I went up to Scotland   to Chris's castle it was like mine oving   identical like a copy but darker

and there was a fire burning in the grate and the room and the light and temperature was freezing there was paltry   light   frighteningly low-lit

the narrow light   what there was of it   was caustic   green it   looked like someone had let out a very sneaky arabesque   fart

that was snaking well-nigh invisibly around this glamorous room

there was a host   of passionate school acquaintances there   who had charcoal faces and hair

and   I recognised them Harry Macadam and
Ian   they all had connections to evil   whoever kept farting

was gay because the emissions were silent and the timing was linked and I got whiff of it first I felt like a detective on the scent of a crime and the more I saw I could see this conspiracy was unsolvable

I didn't hear so much as a pip   I persuaded some of the top dogs to go to the pool

no bugs was my line of persuasion but it started to rain obscuring any bubbles

we kept the fire limping in the grate which had an oenological look, bum-lit   we ran out of wood … … but the whole house was heated on your farts   whosoever you were

and when they opened the French windows onto the lawn it was littered with broken bodies of the deceased statues that had fallen   you billowed out   an ague   a ghost

so Chris sold the house but no one was sure who it was the mr x   it was like a brew of all of us that escaped

for we were all long gone

but no one knew when we'd gone beyond the point say, that   Jonestown was no longer led by Jim Jones.

Mortification of the Flesh Dream

       Dego was being kept alive like a pig from whom they cut a pound of flesh every time they were hungry

    and he had tears on him, maggots like Milkybar chocolate buttons

       he was being kept like a pig and the maid Margarita was saying "you're alright aren't you pig?"

    and he would honk   and

     the father had a dead   older brother from childhood and father had inherited everything after
he died but the bro was kept as a spook   with his

       marvelously   heavy presence

   and he was a   living   foodstuff as well

       and the maid Margarita would tell her friends it was like her own extended snuff movie pay back for what she'd suffered as a maid

       and she'd downgraded him   down so far there was like a magnanimity   a melancholic one

as if she was a Princesse de Luxembourg in Proust feeding the upper middle class family sweets on the beach   like bread to ducks

  or it was as if she had gone   back in time   and had to be careful not to touch too much

   there was a   magnanimity petering out into a carefulness

   and after a while she bred the whole family like that   eating them and keeping them on a chain as her dogs were

     and took over the estancia — like an adjacent town   would want to   usurp the landowners that had founded   it

     a narcissist engulfing everything that reminded her of her own fragility